IF YOU KNOW WHAT I MEAN

cah-PEESH?

John Apicella

Acknowledgements

Paula Radder, these are the words that describe you, and what you did to get this book formatted to publish: Patient, enthusiastic, dedicated, wizard of the key pad, dynamo, geek. Thank you, thank you, thank you.

Marci Davis, it's all your fault. You offered the class at our condo, I participated, you suggested, to be a writer, one should write a little every day, I did and I do. See what you started, thank you.

Donna Charest, classmate, punctuation coach extraordinaire. Thank you.

Florida Classmates, Jessica, Donna, Elliott, Frank, Peter, Bob, Lorraine, Marie, Irene, I thank you for your kind words and encouragement. Your comments, all of which I saved, are appreciated and continue inspiring me to write. By the way, every one of you can do what I did, go ahead, give it a try, Write Away.

Fellow self-publishers for advice and direction, Frank Spera, Florida, Robert Garvey, Kentucky, Thank you.

In Connecticut: Ellen LoGiudice, punctuation. Thank you.

Tom Fitzpatrick, reader, critic, editor, brother, friend. Thank you.

About the title: If You Know What I Mean

The line that appears in many of my stories, and is the title of this book, is a definition of the first Italian word every kid learns, even if he's not Italian.

That word, pronounced, cah-PEESH, is an Italian word used in American slang to say "got it?" or "do you understand?"

"If you know what I mean,"   means,   Get it?   Got it? Good!

CahPEESH?

Contents

Forward

My stories are just like a box of chocolates...you never know what you are going to get. That may not be an original thought but it is a perfect description of what you get reading what I write.

These days everybody is into physical exercise, and that's a good thing. But I think we should also exercise our brain. In the things I write about, and in the way I write about them, I try to cause your brain to get exercise and have fun. Hidden somewhere in my stories is something that will cause the reader to think to himself, "where's this nut case going with this nonsense and what's it got to do with anything, anyway." Then the reader finds that *sometimes it's got nothing to do with anything and sometimes it is the story.*

I've been trying to figure a way I can get a real objective opinion about my writing. To say that the response I've gotten so far is positive and encouraging, would be an understatement.

However the responses are from people who live in my world and with whom I have a relationship of one kind or another. I know they like me. I know I love them. Are they subliminally biased in my direction? Obviously, the very fact that I offered to show my stuff to them, indicated that I thought I had something worth showing and sharing.

I have assembled 40 of my stories and printed them up in this neat little book. It is time to thank the readers who read my stuff along the way, said nice things, and asked to see more. Each one of you, (you know who you are), is the reason I did this. If just one of you, or maybe two of you, had said anything discouraging I probably would have thrown in the towel and found something else to fill my days in the sun.   Maybe take up golf.

Scattered throughout my stories are fictions and facts that will rattle around in your head and get stuck in your brain. Reading my stuff ain't easy. Reading slowly is best; like with stand-up comedy, timing is everything.

The easy part about reading me is that each time you read,

If you know what I mean,

You'll know what I mean.

cah-PEESH?

My First Crack at Story Telling

For my seventh grade English class we were required to get a book from the library, read it, then stand before the class and make an oral report.

To say that I was not much of a student or reader in the seventh grade would be an accurate statement.

Time comes for my turn to step up to the front of the class to give my report. I did get to the library and I do have a book in hand. That much I accomplished.

Unfortunately I never got around to reading that damn book. But I figure there are 36 kids in the class all giving reports on that very day.

And there are hundreds maybe thousands of books in the library, I figure it's not possible that the teacher could possibly have read every one of them.

Standing at the front of the class with the book held up to my chest, with both hands, I proceed to tell the story. I don't remember any of the details but I do remember that at the time I thought I had delivered a very good report.

When the bell rang ending class the teacher told me to remain. Always the optimist I expected to be complimented for my outstanding report.

Either she read that damn book or something about my story didn't ring true. She knew I never read the book and that I made up the story I told.

Well I've been telling stories ever since, mostly true stories. Albert Einstein once said that if everybody's life was like his there would be no need for novels.

Fortunately my real life stories are so good that I'm pretty sure the seventh grade story is the last one I had to make up.

My mother used to say that I'd be able to story my way out of Hell. We'll see about that.

Holy Crap

My friend Bruce is a high roller casino gambler. His game is craps. I share a love of and attraction to the crap table with Bruce.

Recently Bruce and his wife Maria invited Linda and me to join them on a cruise from Barcelona stopping at major ports in Italy including Rome. This was a high rollers cruise attended by other big time gamblers from around the world. I am not in their league.

About a month after I had paid $2,250 for our Norwegian Cruise Line accommodations, I got a call from Bruce. He told me that one of the high rollers in the group owed the casino sponsoring the trip over one million dollars, and they withdrew his comp. The accommodations he was planning to occupy had become available.

The cost for said accommodations was $10,000. However, if I acted immediately I could have it for $4,500. Only $2,250 more than I had already paid. Bruce said, if I didn't take it, he would. Since he and Maria on other occasions had enjoyed such luxury, he offered the deal to me. I acted immediately. The accommodations at the bow of the ship, known as "The Captains Suite", included 3 rooms, two bathrooms, two balconies, 3 TVs, a maid and a houseboy. Also other luxuries too numerous to mention here.

Bruce assigned me to use my contacts in Rome to arrange for a guide to the Sistine Chapel. I located and hired the best. Sir Jon Franco, a retired 80 year old art history professor, was our guide. Listening to Sir Franco, as we toured the Sistine Chapel, gave the feeling like he was there when Michelangelo did the job.

But that's not what this story is about. Sir Franco, who is a Knight of Malta, very connected, had arranged for us to visit the tombs below the Sistine Chapel, an area not open to the public. As we approached the area, he quietly informed me that if we were willing to slip the guard a few euros, we might be able to descend deeper into the tombs to an active excavation site where Saint Peter is actually buried. He suggested 40 euros would do the deal. (Cheap at twice the price.)

Bruce and I know a scam when we see one. But how could we resist the opportunity to tell the story about the time we were scammed in the basement of the Sistine Chapel.

Like I'm doing right here, right now.

Sir Franco shakes the guard's hand, whispers in his ear, and we are OK'd to descend to a lower level. Only two of us at a time, down a metal construction staircase. The guard and Sir Franco stand guard. We are instructed that, when we get to the bottom, we will see another metal staircase up to a small platform and a hole being dug. The only light was a 40 watt bulb hanging off a wire. Very dark. Two of us go down; in less than a minute, we are back up. The other two go down.

4

We are silly, feigning amazement and appreciation for this "rare" chance. Picture the guard: short, chubby, uniformed, a black mustache, right out of central casting. All of a sudden the guard is whisking us out of the area announcing his boss is coming, he will be fired, and we will be arrested if caught in this secret holy place. Actually the guard told us this was a secret sacred holy place.

Scam completed, we escape to the Sistine Chapel courtyard above. Thank God!

OK, all that is background. Here is part of what this story is really about.

Located there in the courtyard is a holy water fountain. The night before both Bruce and I had a bad night at the crap table, I lost $900, he lost $10,000. I told you he is a high roller. We each take the opportunity to soak our right hand under the holy water faucet. We are both right handed. We both roll the dice with our right hand.

Back on the ship that night at the crap table, I had the dice in my right, holy water soaked hand for 45 minutes. Crap shooters know what holding the dice for 45 minutes means. I won $1,200, Bruce $12,000. Thank God!

But here's the real story. One year later I read in the NYT that the new pope had just visited the very same excavation site under Saint Peters. He was the first pope to do so. The site is real. The scam was not.

Holy Crap!

Pope visits St. Peter's tomb under Vatican

Does God Have a Desk?

When I sit by the pool and relax, I wonder about things. I have questions.

Like, does God have a desk? I mean, what does He do all day? Wherever He is, does He even have days and nights? Does He put in an 8 hour day or is He, or She, a 24/7 workaholic? For now, I'll assume He's a guy because in all of the pictures of God I've seen, so far, He's always a guy.

The one thing we can all agree on is that God has a lot to deal with every day and night. It's always day and night somewhere in the world.

Some say God doesn't deal with anything. He just lets whatever happens happen. If that's the case, He doesn't need a desk or a laptop or a secretary or even a pad and pencil.

But He must do something. Even if He just lets things happen, He must notice what's happening. If He notices what's happening, He needs a way to keep track of it all. He needs to keep track so that He can make decisions about who goes where at the end. North or South.

If you know what I mean.

Of course, if He is God, He can keep it all in His head. Imagine every single thing that is happening everywhere all in His memory bank of a brain. Does He even have a brain? Does He even need a brain?

OK, here's another question I have. God has a lot of associates. Until I can think of another term to use for the others who hang around with God, I'll call them associates. Also His Mom and Dad and all the saints we hear about. What do they do all day? Aren't they bored just standing around? Don't you think they would want to help God in at least keeping track of everything that's going on night and day? If God doesn't want or need their help, do you think they feel ignored or useless?

Most saints are in charge of a particular department. At one time Saint Christopher was in charge of the Motor Vehicle Department, but he got cancelled when someone in Rome figured out that when Chris was around there weren't any motor vehicles. Then there was the rumor that he jumped out of any vehicle exceeding the posted speed limit or operated by a drunk driver. Presumably, at the time when his services were most needed.

Here's another thing: my guess is that Mother Theresa is in charge of health and human services for the whole world. Don't tell me she doesn't need lots of help. She is definitely under financed. There must be a million low level saints, CPAs and lawyers, in a back room somewhere dealing with raising funds to keep these operations going and handling complaints.

Do any of these associates ever have anything come up where they need to check with the Boss? There must be something, otherwise they themselves would be Gods and we know that would be a contradiction in terms. In this operation, there can be only one Boss.

OK so let's assume, for this moment of contemplation that God does have things to do every day. Where does He do it? Does God have a desk? Does He have a desk chair; does He sit down or does He work standing up? In pictures, He is mostly standing up tall. Can you even call what He does "work?" He's God, his work can't be work. Although I have heard what God does commonly referred to as "God's Work". Go figure.

Let's say Mother Theresa needs to check with God about something. How does she communicate with Him? Does she need to make an appointment? They must have some system better than email and texting. Mental telepathy at least. Probably faster than the speed of light. Surely a paperless system. No file cabinets.

This whole business is very mysterious. For years I've been hearing about a committee involved in church matters. The Father, the Son and the Holy Spirit. That must be the answer. Here's how they do it. I think.

The Father is the Big Boss. He doesn't do details. He's the chairman of the board, sets policy, initiates and schedules miracles and every 15 or 20 years gets involved in electing a new pope. That's enough for Him; He's like retired. He plays a little golf, (very low handicap/ never loses any balls/ record number of holes in one). He sits around the pool; weather-wise it's always a good pool day.

The associates enjoy a happy peaceful retirement having overcome boredom by being enrolled, automatically upon arrival, in the medical marijuana program. They mostly let whatever happens happen.

If you know what I mean.

(Little known fact: Research from this program confirmed that weed is God's way of saying Hi.) (Old Hippies claim that's why they call it Heaven.)

The Son is the God who takes care of the day to day detail stuff. No need of a desk or anything else, a one man show.

The Holy Spirit is the software system designed to keep straight all the stuff coming and going with unlimited memory bank capacity. This is the Cloud we hear so much about. (I think it's somewhere in Utah.)

Now that I figured this out, I can relax, enjoying a happy peaceful retirement, as I sit by the pool and enjoy the Heavenly Florida Sunshine.

If you know what I mean.

Men and Jeans

Some men wear jeans and some don't. I'm talking blue jeans. I am trying to figure out how this happens.

When I think about certain male friends who don't wear jeans I get a feeling that they have made the right choice. Jeans are not right for them. I can't picture them in jeans. It's just a feeling I get. I'm thinking they wouldn't look good in jeans.

On the other hand, friends who do wear jeans look perfectly like they belong in jeans.

It is possible that the reason I feel this way is because I'm used to seeing the guys who never wear jeans, never wearing jeans.

Some would say the reason the guys who I say are right for jeans look so natural in jeans is because they always wear jeans. Maybe.

But men who are right for jeans sometimes don't wear jeans like when they attend a wedding or are on trial.

If you know what I mean.

So every once in a while you do see jean guys without jeans. But you never see guys who never wear jeans wearing jeans. They can't; they don't own any.

Why, and what does it mean?

The reason I'm so troubled about this is because I can't find any other thing either of these groups have in common amongst themselves. Not politics, not sports, not money, not looks or size. Sometimes age. But age is not a controlling factor.

Perhaps I'm the only one who noticed this but now that I mentioned it you will probably start to notice too. If you figure out something you think will help me understand this phenomenon, let me know.

Email's fine.

Girlfriends and Wives

It's important to get the terminology right when meeting new couples.

Retirees in Florida get to meet a lot of senior citizen Jack and Jills, who may or may not be married. They could actually be living together, in sin. You know what I mean.

After you meet these new old timers, the occasion may occur when it is necessary to refer to Jack and Jill and/or introduce them to others.

It has occurred to me that on those occasions, it is best to assume they are not married when making the introduction.

I suggest, it's OK to refer to Jack's wife as Jack's girlfriend, but it's never OK to refer to Jack's girlfriend as Jack's wife.

If you know what I mean.

In case you don't know what I mean, I'll explain.

Wives shouldn't mind being thought of as girlfriends; indicating old man Jack had a choice, and he picked her, as opposed to Jack's stuck with her his wife. Just a thought.

If the woman with Jack is a girlfriend, likely the last thing she wants is to be Jack's wife, or any body's wife for that matter. She's already been a wife and had enough of that life, thank you, she's trying something new, like Jack.

When you are not sure, go with girlfriend.

Bonus Information about the word *husband*: When referring to the man with the women being introduced, the safest terminology to use is Jill's man. "This is Jill, and her man, Jack." Women of a certain age have had it with husbands. They just want a man… and all men want to be *the man*.

Confirmation! Women are different

Ed. Note: This picture, (soon to be available in wallet size) is on display in my Man Cave Garage at my home in Connecticut. I submit herewith unsolicited comments and reactions noted from various friends, family and acquaintances passing through.

Men of my generation do a double take. At first thinking it's some sort of instruction manual for one of my power tools. On closer examination they just stare at it shake their head and ask for a copy.

Perhaps planning to use it for cover in future conflicts justifying failures to push the right button or properly adjust the knobs. Pleading on those occasions "what do you expect from me, a mere mortal man, with all the possibilities to get it wrong?"

My 25 year old grandson said "Grandpa, I learned this about girls in High School".

My gay male friends just smiled.

A Feminist lawyer I know said it is sexist and threatened to show up at my house with Gloria Steinem to picket my garage.

My guess is that if Bill Clinton and Bill Cosby happened by, their comment would be "No Comment"

Women have suggested adding to the Man Panel buttons switches and knobs to control such things as: attention span, maturity, neatness, a willingness to read instructions, ask for directions and put the seat down. (Among others too delicate to mention here.)

<u>For Men: How To Use This Photo</u>. On those occasions when words or circumstances demand the need to defuse a potential problem, whip out the wallet size, briefly scan the photo as a reminder of what you are up against, then turn it over and respond with words you have chosen to write on the back.

Suggested words: "I'm sorry, you're right, I'll try to do better next time…"

It works every time!

That Clock

In 1976 we took a family trip to California. Me, Linda, and the 3 kids.

We flew into San Francisco, rented a station wagon, and explored. We hit all the tourist spots, like the Redwood Forest and The Golden Gate Bridge.

We slept one night on the Queen Mary, which had been converted into a hotel and went to Yosemite to see Old Faithful and El Capitan.

We visited Tijuana, Mexico, stopped at the mission at San Juan Capistrano and flew home from LA.

Two weeks, 2400+ miles worth, we wandered around California doing touristy things.

But this story is about a clock. That clock.

On the second day of the trip, we are walking on the boardwalk at San Jose Beach. Somehow, I wander into an antique shop and see a clock. I should mention here I am in no way into clocks or antiques. For some reason I noticed that clock. Notice I didn't say I was attracted to that clock, I just noticed it. The asking price was $150. After a few minutes I wandered out of that shop. It's important to note here that the notice I made of that clock when I was in the shop wasn't even a big kind of notice. It was just an ordinary every day kind of notice, the same kind of notice I gave to all the other stuff in that store. Which wasn't much.

You may say what difference does it make, how much notice. So I'll tell you. During the rest of that day I thought about that clock. I thought about that clock a lot. When I went to bed that night, I was still thinking about that clock. The clock that I hardly noticed in the shop.

Next morning I wake up thinking about that clock. As I tell this story, it is occurring to me how ridiculous it should have been at that time for me to be giving that clock a second thought. As I try to put this experience into words for the first time, I'm saying to myself, "what possessed me to notice that clock?" Absolutely crazy.

Of course that morning, I go back to see that clock. While I'm doing this I must have been wondering, what's happening to me to be wasting time going back there. There is no way anything will come of this visit to that clock place. Let me repeat that, THERE IS NO WAY ANYTHING WILL COME OF THIS VISIT TO THAT CLOCK PLACE.

I pause here to catch my breath and collect my thoughts.

I offer the sales girl $90, prepared to increase my offer to $100 in the negotiation I anticipate will take place. That shop girl tells me she has no authority to negotiate. I pay the $150.

Three reasons why this makes no sense: I'm not into antiques or clocks, not then, not now. I really could not afford to spend $150 at that time for that clock. I had to schlep that clock all over California on the floor of the station wagon for the next 12 days and then find a way to get it to Connecticut on the airplane. (We used to say airplane; now we say plane, just thought I should mention that.)

Back in Connecticut, I wind up the clock and hang it on the wall. It's been hanging there for 42 years, keeping perfect time. I remember to wind the clock every 8 to 10 days. Did I mention it keeps perfect time? The time it keeps is so perfect it's spooky.

About 20 years ago it occurred to me the clock may be worth lots of money. It's not. I checked with two antique clock experts; both confirmed the clock is nothing special, just like me, vintage circa late 1930s, just like me, worth about what I paid for it.

There are things about that clock that concern me. Is that clock somehow connected to me in ways I don't understand? There have been times when I forgot to wind it, and it stopped. When I discovered that it had stopped at a particular time, say 10:42, even though I don't know what day it stopped at 10:42, I try to think back to all the recent 10:42s, AMs and PMs, to see if something good or bad happened to me at those times. Nothing.

I'm not superstitious, normally I don't have these kinds of thoughts, but the whole business about what happened with that clock is so contrary and crazy that I can't help but look for some, behind the curtain explanation.

Me and that clock are both of the same vintage, late 30's. Could it be that me and that clock are moving through time together?

I feel a need to keep that damn clock ticking.

I'm wondering if as long as that clock keeps ticking, I'll keep ticking. And when it stops ticking, I'll stop ticking. It has stopped ticking. Some times for a few days when I forgot to wind it, but I kept ticking. That's comforting to know.

When I began to live in Florida for 6 months every year, it occurred to me I should make arrangements to keep that clock wound and ticking. Like hire a clock winding service to come in once a week to wind. Or maybe I should bring it to Florida. I do neither.

I do stop the clock at midnight the day before I leave for the winter in Florida. I am very careful about what I do at midnight when I'm in Florida. Mostly I'm sleeping at midnight.

I figure the only way I will ever know if there is anything to that clock ticking, and the me ticking nonsense, is if I stop ticking at midnight in the winter months while I'm in Florida.

On the other hand, if I stop ticking in the Summer time, note the time and check that clock.

If you know what I mean.

Old Friends

Can you make old friends? You can make new friends anytime. You do so often. But for someone to be your old friend, that friendship had to begin a long time ago. Yes? Maybe!

When I began writing about this, my plan was to tell a story about how one goes about making an old friend.

I figured first you would start with making a new friend. Once that had been accomplished you set in motion regularly planned activities and forms of contact over a period of years, to cement the basic fundamental friendship with the new friend. Then gradually after many years of life you wake up one day and realize you have created and developed into an old friendship. Sometimes that's how it happens.

However most of the time you don't make old friends; old friends just happen; most often completely out of your control and awareness. We commonly refer to friends we've known for many years as old friends, when in fact they are nothing more than regular friends that you have known for many years.

Moving right along here, we now have in the mix three kinds of friends, new, regular and old.

New friends come and go. When you are young you have the time it takes to decide which of the new people you meet will be your new friends. Older people know almost immediately who will make the cut and who won't.

If you know what I mean.

A regular friend you have known for 40 years is not automatically an old friend. Duration is not by itself the controlling factor. If experiencing tough and challenging times together over long periods of time is required then duration is a controlling factor.

The fact is you can't just make old friends, even with a plan to do so. Old friends just happen or they don't and there is not much you can do about it. You might wind up being old friends with someone you would rather not be even regular friends with. You could get stuck with a bad old friend that wasn't even your fault.

If you know what I mean.

For all of my adult years I have pondered about, and marveled at, a particular kind of friendship I have experienced. It's the one where although you have not seen or heard from that friend for a long time, like months or years, and then when you do get together you pick up right where you left off the last time you met or spoke.

When you meet that kind of friend you hug and mutually agree to never let so long a period of time pass until you meet again. And you both really mean you won't let it happen again. But it happens again and again.

In my experience the only thing you can do about the again and again happenings is to cut down the duration between hugs.

Shakespeare said it best:

"Those friends thou hast, and their adoption tried,
Grapple them to thy soul with hoops of steel."

You know what I mean.

My Cousin Vinny

In 1954 before Steve Jobs and Bill Gates were even born, I had a working telephone in my car.

In 1954, I bought a 49 Ford for $240. I was 16, my first car. It had a radio but no heater. Of course no telephone. I am absolutely certain nobody had a car phone in 1954. However, at that time, most cars did have heaters.

I attended a regular high school; Cousin Vinny went to electrician trade school. I bought a used car heater in a junk yard for $12 and together, we installed it in the Ford. So now I had a car with a radio and a heater, no phone. Car phones had not been invented yet. Did I mention it was 1954?

One day, Cousin Vinny and I are playing around in his garage. The garage had a loft. The loft served as our clubhouse, shop and laboratory. We had an old, smelly, cushioned sofa, some tools, a bunch of wires and a box full of old radio equipment and telephone parts. I don't remember the color of the sofa.

Our plan was to build a transmitter and become Ham Radio Operators. That was cutting edge technology in the 50s. With what we had to work with in parts and brains, we were limited. Somehow we were able to put together enough of the wires and parts to get a phone system to work. We were able to communicate from the lower level of the garage to the loft above. For that system, the maximum distance we could communicate was limited by the length of the wire.

But we were determined to get that phone to work in my car.

And we did.

I will explain the technical details later.

Don't forget Bill Gates and Steve Jobs started in their garages.

Once we had the phone working in my car, we decided to demonstrate its operation to our friends. At that time, the place where we hung out was on Paulie's front porch. His porch was about 2 miles from the garage. A very long wire away, indeed. We solved that problem. Stand by, you'll see.

I pull up to the curb in front of Paulie's porch in my Blue 49 Ford, actually it was light blue, 4 door. The driver side window is down so that all could see me holding the phone receiver to my ear talking on the phone. Paulie, Al, and Bobby were on the porch. Paulie noticed first. He approaches the car window. I make like I don't notice him. I continued my conversation. Paulie is patiently waiting for me to finish the call. For reasons I'll explain later, this call must be limited in duration. Paulie continues to just stand there like nothing unusual is happening. Having a working phone in a 49 Ford in 1954 was something Paulie should have marveled at. But he just stood there, like it's normal for someone to be talking on a car phone in 1954.

I know the clock was ticking. I spring into action. I hand the phone to Paulie and say "Vinny wants to say hello." "Make it snappy, we need to get moving." When Paulie hears Vinny's voice on the phone he wakes up and takes notice that he's actually talking to Vinny on a car phone.

He alerts Al and Bobby. They rush to the car window, grabbing for the receiver. They all want to try it. And they do. Time is passing and Vinny is telling each of them to cut it short and give the phone back to John. Finally they do. Vinny's words to me are, "John, let's get moving it's getting hot."

I realize the problem. I grab the phone, start the Blue Ford, and peel away from the curb. I drive one block and around the corner. I'm looking for some place to pull over, where no one will notice me jumping out to open the trunk to let Cousin Vinny out.

Technical details:

We used the smelly cushions from the old sofa to line the car trunk so Cousin Vinny would be comfortable.

We ran the wire from the phone under the front and back seats under floor mats into the trunk.

(I just can't remember the color of that damn sofa.)

The trip from the garage to Paulie's was too long for Vinny to ride the whole way in the trunk. We needed to find a place to stop nearby to get Cousin Vinny in the trunk just before we pulled up to Paulie's porch.

Cousin Vinny got in the trunk around the corner from Paulie's porch. It was a busy neighborhood. I can't recall how we did it. Unnoticed. But we did. Today people would notice when you put someone in the trunk of a car. In 1954, not so much.

(I can't decide, it was 60 years ago, but I'm pretty sure, the 49 Ford, with radio heater and phone, was not regular blue, more like light blue, 4 door.)

Let's Not Get Carried Away

I recall conversations I had in 1978 with Baseball Hall of Famers, Joe DiMaggio and Phil Rizzuto.

I've been a Yankee fan for 70 years. These Italian guys are my heroes.

Perhaps for that reason I never forgot the exact words each of them said to me on those occasions.

Joe was already in the Baseball Hall of Fame and Phil would eventually get there.

As the years passed, from a distance, I came to appreciate what a kind gentleman Phil was. As a longtime fan I listened to a lot of TV and radio broadcasts. Phil was a Yankee color commentator for more than 30 years. Everybody loved Phil. He was the kind of guy you would want to be your Uncle Phil. Phil was just a nice guy.

My conversation with Phil in 78 involved my Aunt Lena, age 85, herself a Yankee/Phil fan. We had occasion to be at a country club where Phil was playing golf. Aunt Lena spotted Phil sitting in his golf cart about to tee off; she wanted to meet him; I ran ahead to ask Phil if he would say hello to Aunt Lena.

Phil's answer to my request was, "where is she?" just as he noticed her about 20 yards away struggling with her walker to get closer. He jumped out of the golf cart running, arms open, toward Aunt Lena shouting, "Aunt Lena, wait, I am so glad to see you," as he gave her a big hug he said "thank you for taking the time to come and say hello to me." Those words, him thanking her. What a guy!

Now Joe is another story. I am at the same golf course this time with my kids, ages 10, 11, and 12.

Its 8 AM. Nobody around. Joe is on the driving range by himself hitting a bucket of balls.

When he finishes he turns, walking toward us, I approach and ask "Joe, can we take a picture?" Without saying a word he obliges, standing behind my 3 kids.

I take the picture. OK, my turn. I hand the camera to my daughter Maria and stand next to Joe to take my picture with him.

I'm standing next to Joe DiMaggio, my right arm around and touching his back, camera clicks, picture taken. To be sure we'd have a good shot I look up at Joe and say, "can we take another?"

I never forgot Joe's 5 word response, or the stern look he gave me as he spoke.

I pause here to report that I have read pretty much everything written about Joe DiMaggio and his relationship with the public: standoffish, very private, not so nice a guy, and always a man of very few words. (I still like him a lot!)

Joe died in 1999. In 2001 Richard Cramer wrote a biography of Joe, The Hero's Life. In that book Cramer wrote, "everyone who ever spoke to Joe

DiMaggio remembers the exact words Joe said to them".

Along with remembering Joe's 5 word response, the other thing I will never forget is what I was thinking standing near and touching Joe. I wasn't thinking about his 56 game consecutive hitting record. I'm thinking, "This guy slept with Marilyn Monroe!"

The 5 words Joe said to me when I asked to take another picture: He looked me in the eye and said "Let's not get carried away."

Flower Lives Matter

Flowers are beautiful, alive with color and fragrance.

A large segment of the population gives and receives flowers as tokens of love and affection. Wonderful.

Beautiful big arrangements and bouquets of flowers adorn wedding tables and church altars. Incredible.

Maybe it's just me but I think flowers belong in the garden.

Cut flowers have a 10 day life. At the precise moment the flower is picked it starts a slow death spiral. It's no longer alive; it wilts, the beauty and color begin to fade.

Now a word about wilting: The very word, wilting, sounds bad. Wilting is the first step toward oblivion for the poor suffering dying flower.

And the fragrance... at some point soon after harvesting the beautiful fragrance starts to move down the road to less fragrance and then no fragrance on the way to smelling bad and finally it stinks.

I'm surprised plants and flowers aren't organized.

Protesting at the local flower shop: "Flower Lives Matter." "Flower Lives Matter."

I love flowers; I just can't understand how killing them caught on as a sign of love and affection.

Here's the answer: even after it dies the flower's beauty lives on in the heart.

Also true of loved ones. That's the connection. I feel better now.

If you agree raise your hand.

FL and CT Bugs

I find that in Florida, biting bugs and mosquitos are much more well behaved than their cousins in Connecticut.

In Florida, it's like the bugs subscribe to a live and let live approach to people. You don't bother them, they don't bother you.

In Connecticut, it's like war.

I think it's because the Florida bugs know their place. They live longer so they are older and wiser. They know enough to bug off.

The pest control business in Florida is strong, working 12 months a year, controlling things. Very aggressive. Pest control in Connecticut, not so much. It's only a problem for about 4 months, then forget about it for 8 months. The pest control industry in Connecticut is weak. Bugs sense this vulnerability.

Bugs in Connecticut are pissed-off because they were born in a place where they have to face winter. Being pissed off all the time makes them crazy, mentally disordered, AKA Buggy. So they fight back. I mean they bite back.

People who are mentally disordered are commonly referred to as being "buggy".

It just occurred to me that must be the origin of the word "buggy".

You think...?

Squirrels Have Nuts. It's a Confidence Thing.

Every once in a while the TV camera at the ball park will zoom in on a squirrel that has run onto the field of play. The announcer may say a word or two about it, fans who notice may murmur or chuckle, but nobody gets very excited and the game plays on.

Now just for a moment think how different the reaction would be if what ran onto the field of play wasn't a squirrel but a rat. Not entirely beyond the range of possibilities. I understand there actually are rats living in the scoreboard at Fenway Park. Yes, that old Green Monster.

Play would stop, players in the area would move away, the grounds crew would likely be engaged, the crowd would go silent and some squeamish fans might even leave the park in haste never to return to that venue.

Although this doesn't happen every day at the ball park it does happen every day at our condo pool. Not rats but squirrels.

Why the difference you ask? It comes down to 2 things. Squirrels show up in the day time, standing there with their cute little paws, munching on their nuts. Squirrels look you right in the eye with that "I'm not afraid of you" attitude because nobody ever tries to exterminate squirrels. Although in my opinion they should.

Rats work nights, sleep late, and only come out when it's dark and no one is around. We never got used to them as kids. And everybody wants to exterminate rats. They should.

The other thing is that squirrels have cute bushy tails, rats have long skinny ugly tails. Bottom line squirrels have nuts; it's a confidence thing. I offer this explanation, in case like me, you have wondered about this.

You know and I know, we both know, that only a certain kind of people wonder along these lines.

If you know what I mean.

The Time I got To First Base at Yankee Stadium

Reggie Jackson hit 4 home runs in four consecutive appearances at the plate. But it's not recorded as such in the baseball record books.

But I know it happened because I was at Yankee Stadium sitting in the same seat for all four homers, and I saw it happen. And it was in conjunction with that event that I, in my capacity as a life-long Yankee fan, season ticket holder, got to first base. I mean the real first base. The one right there on the field. Ninety feet from home plate.

Did I mention it was during the actual game? Well it was. It was Opening Day 1978. How could it be that the fourth consecutive home run was hit in the first inning?

Even a casual baseball fan knows enough about the game to know that it's not possible to come to bat four times in the first inning of a game; even on Opening Day 1978. Everybody knows that's ridiculous.

Not as ridiculous as me getting to the real first base right on the field right after Reggie hit home run number 4.

In case you're wondering that fourth home run was a long low drive over the auxiliary score board into the Yankee bullpen. About 342 feet from home plate. I think it was 342, but it could have been 343 or maybe 350. I can't be sure. It was a long time ago and I'm an old man. But I digress.

I say again, in case you forgot, this is a true and accurate story; every word.

I never said Reggie's 4 consecutive appearances at the plate were in the same game. As a matter of fact those four appearances weren't even in the same season. True and accurate; don't doubt me.

Ok, I'm ready to spill the beans; here is how it happened. In the last game of the 1977 World Series Reggie hit 3 home runs in his last three times at bat. The Yankee's won the series and Reggie was the star.

Perhaps you have heard of Babe Ruth. Surely you know there is a Baby Ruth candy bar. I will check to see if that candy bar was named after Babe Ruth.

Now you ask what a candy bar has to do with me getting to first base in the first inning of the Opening Day game at Yankee Stadium in 1978. You'll never guess, so I'll tell you now.

Reggie's stardom resulted in the birth of a candy bar named for him. On opening day 1978 everyone entering the stadium was handed a Reggie Bar.

The Reggie Bar was round in shape. About 3 inches in diameter, just the right size to fit between your thumb and forefinger. Perfect for flinging like a miniature Frisbee. That Reggie Bar got me to first Base on Opening Day.

When Reggie came to bat in the first inning, his first time at bat in the 1978 season, he hit a home run. Don't forget he hit home runs in his last three at bats of game seven of the 1977 World Series ending that season. So just like I said he hit 4 in a row.

The fans in the stadium went nuts as Reggie rounded the bases. About the time he got to the first base bag, in his home run trot, Reggie Bars began flying onto the field. Remember I said the Reggie Bar fit perfectly between the thumb and forefinger. Perfect for flinging from the stands. The candy bar was soft enough so even if you got hit in the head with one you would probably not bring suit. But you never know about things like that.

Imagine circular candy bars flying onto the field from all directions. The field is littered with thousands of bars. It definitely was thousands because what happened next is how I got to first base.

The stadium grounds crew came out onto the field with dozens of empty five gallon buckets. I see they are allowing fans onto the field to assist in the clean-up operation. This sounds crazy; today if you step one foot over the rail onto the field you're busted and jailed by the cops.

My season ticket box seat is in the first row right next to first base. The Yankee grounds crew is overwhelmed. Realizing this was my chance to get to first base, I hop over the rail, I'm on the field, right near first base, bucket in hand, picking up Reggie Bars.

Cleanup completed, I make it a point to step on first base on my way back to my seat.

Doorbell Ringtone Fun

In my experience, the only cell phone ringtone that gets everybody's attention is the doorbell ringtone. Long ago, before I realized the implications, I chose the Doorbell Ringtone for my iphone.

Now I understand you may not have experienced this attention getter because you have never known anyone who chose that particular ringtone.

In case you are thinking you must have known someone with that ringtone, you just don't remember hearing it, you're wrong. If you heard it, you'd remember it. Don't doubt me on this.

Whip out your cell phone, go to Sounds, scroll to Doorbell and listen. Am I right? Like I said, you never heard it before!

I've actually been visiting friends who got up to answer the door when my phone rang. It's happened to me in my own house, and it's *my own ringtone.* On occasion I actually move toward the front door of my house before I realized it is my phone ringing. Go figure! I know what you are thinking....

Moving right along here, let us consider who would choose such a ringtone, and why!

For my ponderings on this subject I did some research. You can do the same research. Return to the ringtone menu. You have more than 50 to choose from; index finger ready, let's start from the top. Let's listen to each of the ringtones together.

You don't have to use your index finger. You can use any finger you want. It's a free country! I just happen to use my index finger because that happens to be one of my smartest fingers. Back in the day, I used that finger to dial phone numbers. I figure I dialed that way for 20 years, 2500 calls per year, that's 50,000 times I used that finger, probably more.

I'm not just talking about touch tone dialing where all you had to do was touch the number on the phone button. I'm talking about the days when you actually had to put your finger in the right hole on the dialer and then bring that hole around to the stopper, then pull your finger out of that hole and wait for the dialer to go back to the start position. Then that index finger had to find the next number hole. Hole after hole seven times. You think that was easy? It's good that there were no area codes in those days because then you need to find 10 holes. I digress.

OK, we've listened together to all the ring tones on our cell phones. What a waste of time. Here's what we learned: we learned that all other ringtones are equal and ordinary. As a matter of fact to my ear, most of them are downright annoying.

When those ordinary ring tones ring, the owner of that phone notices and answers.

When that doorbell ringtone rings, everybody notices and reacts in some way... and that's fun.

I have determined that, people who choose the doorbell ringtone are people who just want to have fun.

Tell Me No Secrets

If you have any secrets, don't tell them to me. Please.

Every once in a while someone will blurt out something to me and then say, "Please don't tell anyone." "It's a secret and I don't want anyone to know."

Let's get something straight, I have no interest in hearing anything from this person in the nature of personal and/or "not for publication" information.

Chances are that I have no interest in hearing anything of substance from this particular person about anything. The last thing I want is to be placed in a position where I may conceivably be suspected of being the one who "spilled the beans" when word of this secret gets out, as it always does.

I wonder why if they don't want anyone to know, why are they telling me. Am I someone who is not an anyone?

My concern is that if they are telling me, they are telling others. When word gets out about whatever it is they don't want revealed, I could wind up being the one blamed, even though I would never tell.

I work hard at not knowing too much about the people I know, so that I will never be in a position to reveal anything about them that isn't already known by everyone else in the group.

If you know what I mean.

In regard to these matters, it is a well-known fact about me that I don't do details. I make it a point to not pay close attention to what's going on in group conversations and discussions. I'm likely to pick up enough of what's being said to get the big picture. This works for me because the big picture is what everyone already knows.

Get it? Got it! Good.

Wrinkles & Spots

Do you ever notice wrinkles in people's clothes? Maybe it's just me, but I don't notice if someone is wearing a wrinkled garment. I agree everybody has wrinkles. Unless you just stand up straight, and hardly move about after putting on a neatly pressed garment, you will get wrinkled. I actually know a woman who will not wear a car seat belt, because she is concerned about wrinkling her outfit. She's willing to risk her life to avoid wrinkles.

Chances are, now that I mentioned it, you will begin to notice that generally you do not notice wrinkles. Generally men don't, women do. What I'm telling you here is that if you are a woman who notices wrinkles you will just go on noticing like you always have. Same for men who notice wrinkles. The few men who do, likely only notice a few and then only the really big ones.

Because we are having this discussion, those who do, and those who don't, and those that do just a few, will all increase their noticing of wrinkles. You will not be able to control yourself, when the next wrinkled one shows up, you'll notice.

When you notice wrinkles, I suggest you keep it to yourself. Nobody wants to hear about someone else's wrinkles, and of course never mention your observation to the wrinkled one.

The very same inspectors who do wrinkles are likely also noticing spots. The most common spot noticed by spot spotters is the shirt spot. Shirt spots are the most obvious spots to notice, because they are right out there up front, just below eye level.

Most often shirt spots are centrally located about half way down on the shirt. Shirt spots usually result from food or drink spilling, splashing, leaking, dribbling, overflowing and falling over the lower lip, dropping to the chin, from where it is launched onto the shirt, usually in a direct line with the nose and chin. Centrally located shirt spots are the second most famous and well noticed. The most noticed of all time are pants spots.

If you know what I mean.

I imagine there are some spots I will notice. Like a big red spot, on a white shirt, near the heart, right next to what looks like a bullet hole burn. Chances are I will notice that spot. You can be sure if I noticed that particular kind of big red spot I'd ask about it. I mean how often do you see something like that right out in the open and be in a position where you can go right up to the guy with the spot and ask, hey, what happened to you?

Of course it goes without saying that you can only make that inquiry of the guy, with the big red spot on the white shirt, if he's vertical.

If you know what you mean.

Toilet Seats

When's the last time you gave any thought at all about the toilet seat you use every day of your life. People live in the same house for years and never give replacing the toilet seat a second thought.

You never hear about anybody trying out a toilet seat before purchasing one. You are encouraged to test drive a car before buying. You can live together with someone to try out marriage. A lot of marriages don't last as long as toilet seats. Just saying. You can return a mattress after 30 or 90 days if it's not right for your back, but I bet you never heard of anybody returning a toilet seat because it didn't fit their ass comfortably.

At Home Depot there are more than 40 toilet seat styles and sizes on display. No free trials; you use it you own it.

You may say comfort is not a factor because you don't sit there that long on any given day. Well you should sit there longer. Sitting and relaxing for longer periods is good for you. It will help you produce, propel and deliver according to my mom.

If you know what I mean.

In the future, when traveling or visiting friends, try different toilet seats. When you start to pay attention you may find something more comfortable than the one you have at home.

If that happens take a picture of it with your phone. Use that photo when shopping for a new toilet seat. A good one costs less than $100.

Rarely does one get to experience exactly what they are reading about while they are reading about it. Since it has been mentioned that this book belongs in the toilet, you may, while reading this, be enjoying one of those rare experiences.

How nice and convenient is that?

If you know what I mean.

Mom's Medical Advice

When my mother was a young girl, she wanted to become a nurse.

Her father refused to allow her to pursue her dream because he said he didn't want his daughter wiping patient's asses. It was 1930, I'm sure it was men's asses he was concerned about. For her entire working life, she was a seamstress working in a dress shop. She enjoyed her work and was well paid. As far as I know the only asses she ever wiped besides her own was mine.

I submit these facts as background. Mom had no medical training but she did dispense medical advice to me, and I am prepared and willing to share it here with you.

Mom was convinced eating raw carrots was good for your eyesight; I ate a lot of raw carrots. Fortunately I liked carrots. Still do.

She claimed that every hour of sleep you got before midnight counted as two hours. I think she invented that one as her way to convince me to get enough sleep voluntarily because, even as a very young child, I never had a bedtime.

Whenever anyone was having a bad day physically or mentally, mom knew the plain and simple reason was because they had gotten up on the wrong side of the bed that morning. (I guess this reasoning only applies if you sleep alone.)

These days we hear a lot about the benefits of Omega 3 and fish oil. I guess my mom was on the cutting edge of medical science back in the 1940's because she made sure that every day of my childhood, until I was about 10, I swallowed a teaspoon full of cod liver oil. Yuck!

I'm almost 80 now and I have enjoyed a pretty healthy life. I fancy myself healthier than most of my peers. Could be mom knew something about fish oil. I still do fish oil every day, not the cod liver kind.

Here's one of mom's remedies you may have trouble believing. I developed a wart about the size of ½ of a pea on my right thumb just above the nail. Every once in a while I bit it off. It didn't hurt. But it always grew back.

One day mom suggested I pee on it. I know what you're thinking. Just because I said it was the size of ½ of a pea, you think her instruction to me to pee on it is somehow a play on the words pea and pee. Well you are wrong. Pea and pee just happen to be similar words; like for this story, sort of a coincidence.

I thought about describing the wart size as like about the size of the eraser on a pencil. But I decided against that because a pencil eraser size is about twice the size of this particular wart. If you make a lot of mistakes when writing with a wooden pencil and you use the eraser a lot and you wear down the eraser to about half the size it is when the pencil is new, then that eraser is down to the size of my wart.

I gave it a lot of thought and decided it would be easier to describe the size of the wart as being like ½ of a pea. Everybody knows how big a pea is. Maybe I should say how small a pea is. Anyway, if you take a pea and cut it in half with a sharp knife into two halves, one of those halves is about the size of this particular wart. The reason you need a sharp knife is because if the knife is not sharp, it will likely squash the pea when you try to cut it in half and you won't get two perfect halves.

If you know what I mean.

I know you are probably wondering where can I get one pea to cut in half even if I have a really sharp knife. I don't expect you to open a whole can of peas to get just one pea out to work with. Now that I think of it, my experience with canned peas is they are pretty mushy and hard to cut in half.

But what you can do is go to a quality fresh food vegetable market that sells peas that are still in the pod. When nobody is looking, sneak one pea out of a pod. Or if you don't want to be sneaky, you can buy some pea pods. Likely you need to buy a half pound. I don't think you can buy just one pea pod because pea pods are sold by weight and one pea pod doesn't weigh enough to figure out how much to charge for it.

Better to be sneaky. While you are at it, take the whole pod because in the cutting process you will likely squash a couple of peas until you get the hang of it. Especially if your knife isn't real sharp.

You know what…it just occurred to me that the best way to get a good half of a pea would be to use frozen peas because a pea that is frozen solid would be hard to squash even if your knife isn't too sharp.

A word of caution here about getting just one frozen pea to work with. When you open a package of frozen peas, they are all stuck together. If you wait too long before breaking off one of the frozen peas, it will be mushy just like the canned peas. On the other hand, you can't use a pea that is too frozen because it will fracture into a bunch of pieces when you try to cut it. When dealing with frozen peas timing is everything.

Better to stick with the pea pod approach.

That should do it. Now you know the size of my wart. In case you forgot it's on my right thumb just above the nail.

Well it took me a while to take mom's advice, but when I finally did pee on that ½ pea size wart, it worked. I can't remember if I peed on it more than once or how long it took for the peeing to work, but it did work, and the wart never grew back.

Mom knew her stuff.

When I was a kid the most dreaded childhood disease was Polio. My cousin Nick contracted Polio and was crippled for life. Nobody knew what caused Polio. Houseflies were near the top of mom's list of possible causes. The flat we lived in was on the third floor and mom thought that was better than the lower floors because it would be harder for houseflies to get up to our floor. Also if they did make it up to our place, they would be tired and less likely to do harm.

Mom knew how to handle a fly swatter. If there was a Hall of Fame for fly swatters, mom would have been inducted. She was especially good a swatting flies in midair, especially the tired ones that had made it all the way up to the third floor.

At the very top of mom's list of what caused polio was germs. Germs were all over the place and on everything; as far as mom was concerned everything caused polio.

In case you forgot all this was happening during the 1940s. We were at war. We were at war with Germany. If you didn't see it coming, here it is. As a 6 year old, I somehow mixed up germs and Germany. As far as I was concerned, germs and Germany were the same thing and winning the war would be the end of polio.

Somehow Mom and I made it through to Doctor Jonas Salk's discovery of the polio vaccine and mom calmed down.

Mom was also a big believer in bed rest as a cure for any illness. Her advice to anyone experiencing any illness including even a common head cold was, "You should be in bed with a nurse." As a young man I had plenty of head colds. I certainly was willing to take that advice but I didn't know any nurses.

If you know what I mean.

The First Color TV Set

In 1950 I was 12 years old, and we got our first TV set. It was a Ratheon 12 inch round screen. I don't remember how much it cost, but whatever it was it was a lot for my widowed, seamstress mom, to come up with.

We lived in a third floor cold water flat. Frank Palmeri owned the house; he lived on the second floor, and his married daughter lived on the first floor. All were nice people.

The monthly Social Security check we received after my dad died in 1946 was $18. The monthly rent was $12.

We were poor, but I didn't know it because somehow mom made sure I never noticed. A loving extended Italian family helped.

Frank Palmeri had two landlord rules that I can remember. He would not allow mom to buy a Bendix washing machine because the Bendix spin cycle caused severe vibration. Since we were on the top floor, he apparently felt that spinning vibration would shake the building off of its foundation. In those days, understandable.

The other rule, no TV antenna on the roof. I should mention the Palmeri's did not have a Bendix or a TV.

All of this, so far, is by way of background, and as a matter of fact, you don't even need this background but I throw it in to add color and length to the story about our color TV, in 1950.

It is safe to say nobody had a color TV in 1950 because color TV had not yet been invented. Actually, it had been invented but nobody in America had one. But we had one. I'll explain.

Mom bought the TV from Randy's Radio and TV store right around the corner in our neighborhood. I remember the day Randy delivered our set. He hooked up the rabbit ears antenna and offered basic directions.

In his final instruction, he directed our attention to wires located and visible in the back of the TV. There were four unconnected wires sticking out of the control box. He pointed out that although they were unconnected to anything, they were ready to be connected when the time came for them to be connected. Each of the wires was a different color. One was red, one was blue, one was yellow and one was green.

Randy told me and mom that, as soon as color TV became available we should call him, and he would come right over from his store, right around the corner in our neighborhood, hook up the green, red, blue and yellow wires, and our black and white TV would become a color TV.

Randy told mom she shouldn't tell anyone about this high tech feature on our TV set because if word got out about this everyone would want one, and there were only a few available in the entire country. It was only because of Randy's special connections at the Ratheon Company that he was able to get his hands on a few of them.

If you know what he meant.

Uncle Joe

My frugal Uncle Joe took me and his 3 kids to Yankee Stadium for the first time when I was 10 years old.

I stress Uncle Joe was a frugal man. He was also Irish, very religious; the first non-Italian to marry into our very Italian family. He held a middle management position at the US Post Office from which he retired after 40 years. He also collected stamps.

He married my mother's sister, much to the dismay of my maternal grandparents. In the 1930's, Irish and Italians were not the best of friends. However my grandparents grew to love and honor him; he became their favorite son-in-law. Perhaps because he held a job, was frugal, and went to church a lot. I doubt they even knew he collected stamps.

But, I digress; none of this has anything to do with my trip to Yankee Stadium. It does serve however to make a short story longer.

Uncle Joe was a Cleveland Indians' fan. The games we went to each summer were always weekday double headers with the Indians.

Two games for the price of one. I repeat, two games, the ultimate bargain.

Uncle Joe was a nice man with lots of rules and regulations. Included in the regulations was the requirement that, we pack and bring into the stadium our lunch. OK, I can live with that. The rule I report about here is the one dealing with when we could eat that packed lunch.

Uncle Joe ruled that we could only eat that lunch between games of the doubleheader. No eating during games.

I guess his reasoning was that with a good breakfast kids could get through game one, and then eat the packed lunch between games; that would hold us over until we got home for dinner. That worked for his kids who I should mention were girls 10 and under. Me, boy 10, not so much.

Employing these rules and regulations eliminated any need for Uncle Joe to spend money at refreshment stands.

My mom didn't know much about baseball, but she knew boys eat hot dogs at ball games. Also, mom knew Uncle Joe. She always took care to be sure I had money in my pocket to spend on refreshments.

How could I use my money without causing trouble and conflict for Uncle Joe and my girl cousins? No problem. Whenever I left the group on the way to the bathroom, I'd grab a hotdog with mustard, gobble it down, take care of business and rush back to my seat. It always worked. Although Uncle Joe might have caught on because on one occasion, when I got home Mom noticed a big mustard stain on my shirt and another on my chin.

Did I mention that the packed lunches did not include any drinks? They have water fountains for drinking at Yankee Stadium.

If you know what I mean.

The Grandfather Card

Being a Grandfather has its advantages. The more you do it, the better you get at it. I have 25 years of experience in the roll of Grandpa; that's what my granddaughter and grandson call me. Every time I hear them speak that word, my heart skips a beat; I could never hear it enough. Grandpa! Wow!

What I learned about being a Grandfather is this: when grandchildren are born, you are there just a step behind Mom and Dad. Almost like looking over their shoulder. Each year you take a step back. Baby steps back until about Junior High. Then the steps back and away get bigger and faster. The love and concern, however, grows in the opposite direction.

If you know what I mean.

I haven't decided yet whether it's the concern or the love that drives you nuts. I just decided, it's both. Especially around 16 and it never stops.

Bottom line, stand back and let them happen. Enjoy and encourage every accomplishment. Be prepared to support and direct and have the wisdom to know the difference. Remind them that in life it's *the risks not taken that are the most regretted*.

However, none of this has anything to do with The Grandfather Card.

About ten years ago I discovered that old men, Grandfathers, say over 70, have at their disposal, should they choose to play it... The Grandfather Card, (GFC).

I don't mean to imply that any old Grandfather can get into Columbia or Harvard, just by playing a silly card.

If you know what I mean. But I digress.

What I'm talking about here is using age, experience and the accumulated wisdom of many years to get special treatment in life's every day activities.

Wow, special treatment, that's not fair. Just because you got old you want to cut the line. No, no, no, the special treatment I'm after is the kind of treatment everybody used to get back in the day: help, answers, empathy, patience, manners, kindness, and a returned phone call.   Nothing unfair about that.

For example, I use the GFC when I am speaking, usually on the phone, to a Customer Service Representative (CSR) about any business or service matter. The conversation goes something like this:

Me, speaking slowly and clearly, I say, "Good morning, I have a bit of a problem; I hope you can help me." (Speaking slowly and clearly is very important; with the opening words my purpose is to set the tone for the pace of the conversation).

Then I say, "Before I tell you my problem or ask my question, I want you to know I'm an old man and I don't hear very well." At this point the CSR is very likely to say something to the effect that they completely understand. Great, now I have their attention. Hopefully they have concluded this call will be friendly and maybe even fun.

Next, "Do you have a Grandfather?" I ask.

Usually the answer is yes; everybody has a grandfather. Everybody wants to talk about their Grandfather. Almost everybody loves their Grandfather. Now I really have their attention and we are family. This is so easy and fun.

Continuing, I say, "Thank you, I appreciate your help...just talk to me like you would talk to your Grandfather." By this time I'm on a roll for sure. Most CSRs are bored with the job and love having some fun and smiles with a caller. That's me, just having fun.

What Grandfathers can accomplish playing the GFC is attention and help. I actually had a CSR call me back on her day off, as she promised, to solve my cable bill problem.

What you have done is play the GFC. Good show!

The GFC has other uses. A major segment of the population is convinced old men can't hear too good, and they forget a lot. Now we are talking about my favorite use of the GFC.

These are my all-time all-purpose favorites. You can use them in concert or on their own. Nobody expects old men to hear or remember anything. Except maybe your wife, but there is nothing I can help you with in that department.

Wives hear everything, forget nothing. Just saying.

The GFC, for hearing and memory issues, works every time because nobody, again, except your wife, would call you out if you forget or failed to hear something.

What are they going to say? "What are you deaf ?" or worse, "Are you losing your mind?...You must have Alzheimer's." Not likely!

Other benefits of being an old man include getting a handicap parking permit. That permit is a state issued Grandfather Card. I got mine when I had my back surgery. I didn't ask for it. The doctor offered and I accepted. I don't feel I really need it, but I use it when it's raining or when I don't feel like walking far or when I need to load the car.

I will tell you this, when I pull into a handicap spot, and I notice somebody who I think will notice me, as I exit my sporty red convertible, I make it a point to limp a little...just in case. Actually these days I limp a little when I get out of any car even when nobody is noticing.

If you know what I mean.

Girls Don't Spit

Did you ever wonder why you rarely see women spit? Well I have. And this concerns me. What if it turns out that spitting is healthy for women, but men are keeping spitting all to themselves as part of the war on women. The next thing you know "Spitting Women Matter" will be marching.

Likely some Think Tank is studying this very subject. Until we get the official report let me spit out a few words on the subject.

Without giving much thought to it men just spit. Most spitting takes place outdoors: On playing fields, working in the yard, and out the car window, are some common venues for spitting. It's kind of natural and easy for boys and men to spit while peeing. Not so much for girls and women.

If you know what I mean.

Men and boys don't think about spitting even as they are spitting. They don't even think about it after they spit. Unless of course, the spit misfires and hits someone or something unintended.

Women, however would think about spitting before spitting. Thinking about spitting before spitting takes time. Even a few seconds is enough time to reconsider all implications and swallow. Women are much deeper thinkers when it comes to things like spitting.

Another factor, the quantity of spit girls have available is probably a lot less than the amount men generate. This of course is conjecture on my part. I have no way of knowing for sure, but I'll ask around and let you know. If you have time do your own research. It can't hurt.

Another reason girls don't spit is because in most cases, they don't have the kind of spitting power it takes to get the distance needed. Spitters don't want it dribbling down their chin. And what about the aim? To expectorate correctly, you need power and accuracy. When spitting it's important to hit the target or at least come close. Accomplished spitters know before letting go, the volume and target and just what kind of power is needed to reach that target. Wind velocity is sometimes a factor to be considered, especially when spitting into the wind or from a moving car. Always be sure the car window is down. For sure.

Never spit into the wind or text while driving.

Some people ask how do you learn how to spit? Do Dads take their sons to the park when they are about 7 or 8 for "the talk" about spitting. I have never heard of any sons getting "the talk" on this subject.

In my opinion the most accomplished spitters are boys and men who at a very young age started watching baseball being played on real grass fields. I say real grass fields because artificial turf isn't sufficiently absorbent for spitting. Baseball players spit the most. These days they spit out the pumpkin seeds they munch on while on the bench. Regular spitting is mostly done when they are in the field.

The best spitters were baseball old timers who chewed tobacco. If you want to get really good at spitting, I suggest you start chewing. After about two weeks you will be real good at spitting. When I say real good at spitting, I'm not talking about just plain ordinary spitting. I mean the large volume of foul tasting smelly juicy brown liquid you evacuate from your mouth with a force that lands with a splash.

A word of caution here: you should never attempt to hit a target with tobacco juice. That kind of spit is too voluminous and juicy, it will spray all over the place, and some of it will drip down your face and spot your shirt. For all these reasons baseball players stopped chewing tobacco and started chewing bubble gum.

It goes without saying that chewing tobacco never caught on much with girls and women. This factor stunted their spitting development.

Back in the day spittoons were available to accommodate spitters spitting. I can remember the last time I saw a spittoon; it was in my Uncle Mike's barbershop in 1947. That spittoon was a twelve inch round metal bowl with a shiny copper removable top part. That top part was removable so you could clean the spit out and wash it. Well anyway that shiny top part had a 3 inch diameter round hole so a standing man could spit into it. I don't recall ever seeing it being used, but my guess is that it would be necessary for a man to lean over to spit down into it.

From the mouth of a man of average height to hit that 3 inch hole, the spit would travel about 5 feet. Of course the force used when spitting into an appliance of this kind is different than the force used when spitting for distance.

If you know what I mean.

It was on the floor next to the sink. Even though I never saw anyone spit into that spittoon, I'm sure it was used because I do remember seeing it loaded with spit and there were always wet spots on the floor where the spittoon sat.

Spittoon; there's a word that really sounds like what it is and does. I love that word, Spittooooon.

Now in case you haven't noticed football players almost never spit. I suspect there are two main reasons. For obvious reasons they would have to take off their helmet to spit unless they were willing to chance some getting on the face guard. More likely it's because they roll around on the field a lot; need I say more? This is even more of an impediment on less absorbent artificial turf.

To be perfectly honest about spitting, I'm glad women and girls don't spit much. Watching women spit is no fun for me, especially women in heels.

If you know what I mean.

Go Fish

A word of caution: Please don't read this as a knock on the Roman Catholic religion. I will have enough to answer for when I get to the Pearly Gates, without throwing more coals on the fire.

If you know what I mean.

My intention with this piece is to comment on and discuss some basic facts.

I am surprised to find that very few Catholics are aware that the twelfth century doctrine establishing priestly celibacy had nothing to do with sex.

In Europe in the twelfth century the church owned a lot of land. Before they put a stop to it, clergy were getting married and having kids. When the clergyman died his wife and kids got the land.

The whole thing about priestly celibacy is nothing more than a part of a real estate land deal.

Easy problem to solve if you prevent clergy from marrying you prevent legitimate children from being born.

Clergy sex was OK as long as any resulting kids were bastards. Some bastards tried to get land, but the pope nipped this in the bud "bastardizing the bastards" by rigging the system to ostracize them from society for 700 years.

Eight hundred years later clergymen no longer own the church land, but priests still can't marry. Strange but true.

OK here is another aspect of Catholicism a lot of people are unaware of. The obligation to attend Sunday Mass under penalty of Mortal Sin was a marketing program instituted to build attendance.

Before the Mortal Sin Doctrine was introduced attendance was way down, especially in bad weather.

As soon as word about Mortal Sin got out attendance shot through the roof. That's why church ceilings are so high. From now on any time you are in a church with a high ceiling you will remember what you learned here.

Then about the time of the turn of the century, 2000, the pope realized telling people they would burn in Hell for skipping mass was nonsense and likely not enforceable. They decided to gradually phase out the Mortal Sin part, without actually making an announcement. It's been years since I heard anyone say that failure to attend mass is a Mortal Sin.

So what happened? Attendance is way down. Only old people attend mass. They learned about the Mortal Sin part as children. They can't get it out of their head that there may be something to it. So they still show up, but generally attendance is way down along with church ceilings.

Here's another thing that changed. Remember back in the day it was The Father, The Son and The Holy

Ghost? Well when's the last time you heard mention of the Holy Ghost? The church adapted. A focus group of Cardinals met in the Sistine Chapel and came up with the Holy Spirit. As far as I know there was no announcement about this change. It just happened, miraculously. The Holy Ghost disappeared.

If you know what I mean.

Holy Spirit is something you can work with. Like Team Spirit. Team Spirit is good, it could help with attendance. Now all we need is a good coach. But I digress.

While I'm at it, what about the thing about not eating meat on Friday? The Friday fish thing was a marketing plan developed by members of the church who were fisherman looking to sell more fish.

The fact that one of the fishermen could walk on water also helped operations. His services were so much in demand that he partnered with a guy in Rome, did an IPO and franchised.

New rule: No meat on Friday, eat fish. Why Friday you say? Most fish are caught early in the week. Fishing boats get back to the docks Thursday afternoon. Get your fresh fish late Thursday or early Friday.

Little known fact: The words, "Go Fish" did not come about in connection with the card game we all played as kids. No. No. No.

Go Fish was the earliest known marketing slogan.

Signs all over the kingdom read....... Friday? Go Fish.

AMEN

Remote Danger

There is one thing that every man, woman and child on the surface of planet Earth has been effected by for the past 25 years.

Isn't it probable that our brains are in some way being affected by electronic signals being sent through the air every minute of every night and day? Imagine if through the use of some tracer technology, you could see all that traffic displayed on a screen.

Back in the day, electronic signals were sent through wires. You could see the wire, and you knew that whatever was inside that wire would stay inside that wire until it got to where it was going. No way was that, whatever you call it, getting out of the wire to impact your brain.

Concern about the stuff inside the wire getting out and hurting somebody is the reason most wires were hidden in the wall, high up on utility poles or deep underground.

You may be having trouble digesting all this technical jargon, but the one thing we can all agree on is that there's a lot of electronic stuff passing through our brains every day. Need I mention that a lot of this stuff has nothing to do with me and my remotes or you and your remotes.

What if every time my neighbor opens his garage door my brain takes a hit. I know a guy who came home from work one day and discovered that the fireplace in his bedroom was lit. He concluded his wife was having an affair with a neighbor, and forgot to turn off the remote controlled gas fireplace when her lover left. Later he found out that his garage door remote also turned on the fireplace. They divorced anyway. I guess there were other problems in the marriage. But I digress.

Now you may think I'm convinced that all this electrical transmission assaulting our brains is harming us. I'm not sure harming is the right word. The word that applies is impacting. The other word that needs some attention here is stimulation.

What if we are all just getting stoned on remote transmissions, and we don't realize it because it's happening to everyone simultaneously and fast. What if this assault on our brains instead of getting us stoned is making the entire population of the world dumber by the day, and so fast we don't even notice. The reason why we haven't been warned is because the experts who used to warn us about things like this are also dumber. What if it turns out that the smartest are the ones who get the dumbest fastest? Just saying.

Tell me if you agree that every single person in the whole world is in one way or another nuttier than they were 25 years ago. Nothing is the same as it was before we had remote control devices. Every aspect of existence is changed some for the better, but most not so good.

The perfect word to describe the world today is, "nuts." If you can think of a more perfect word, let me know. Sometimes being nutty is fun. My concern is that after "nuts" comes "crazy," and that's no fun.

If you know what I mean.

Let us examine what's cooking in the high tech world. The remote action assault is, of course, also cooking the brains of high tech people. To them it's beneficial stimulation. Bill Gates and Steve Jobs already had super charged brains. Their brains were shovel ready to take off from the inflowing electrons.

Think about how they started and improved over time as their brains got more stimulated by the constant signals bouncing around in their noggin. Gates and Jobs are just two examples of a whole generation of super charged tech brains. They don't notice what's happening. They are too busy creating new and better brain stimulating stuff. Has anyone mentioned addiction?

Each day the body's 37 trillion cells go through countless permutations and transformations; there must be something going on. I'd be remiss if I failed to mention the hundreds of billions of cells in our brain taking hits.

Remote controlled electronic signals passing through, stimulating my brain, is the reason I am able to notice and write about stuff like this.

My brain welcomes the opportunity to share it with your brain.

Mean I what know you.

Are We Having Fun Yet?

Here's another question I've been pondering as I sit by the pool.

What is the answer to the question, "Are we having fun yet?"

This is not a simple question. There are many factors to be considered, not the least of which is how many participants are involved in the event. If there is just one, you yourself, then you can decide without much thought if you have arrived at the fun part of whatever it is you are planning to enjoy AKA having fun. What that means is that if you are the only one participating in the fun then you don't even need to ask the question about the fun. What you are dealing with here is anticipation of the fun. I'm checking with Carly.

If you know what I mean?

On the other hand, if there are two or more people involved is it necessary for all participants to declare in the affirmative? My guess is that with just two involved you would need both to agree. If the group included five people would a simple majority suffice?

Is it possible for three out of five to have fun if two were not ready to participate? Not likely. Especially if one or more of the naysayers has a strong preference for doing something else at that particular time and place.

Another concern I have is how to deal with the problems that arise when at first all agree they are having fun until one or more of the partiers decides they are in fact not having fun and wish to end the festivities or make major changes in the plan. The question now is, if at the outset all agreed they were having fun, can that agreement be cancelled? Is that cancellation retroactive? If retroactive, does that mean nobody had any fun even though before the cancellation they thought they were having fun? Does the fun they thought they just had disappear off the face of the earth? Let's face it with fun, you either have it or you don't. If you had it, no retroactive cancellation is going to take away the fun already had. Even the one who cancelled the fun owns the fun they had right up to the moment of cancellation. Unless the fun they were having before cancelling was fake fun; that's what I call no fun.

Some readers may wonder why I am so concerned and delve into this esoteric question. Although nobody, until now, me, talks about it, this question is on everybody's mind all the time. However, it is only now that I can devote the time and attention to properly address this pressing matter. Retirees by virtue of their life experiences and accumulated wisdom have time to devote to ponderings of this kind.

I have a call into Carly to discuss the question. It is with anticipation that I await her return call. In the meantime, yes, I'm having fun, yet again!

If you know what I mean.

Save Your Breath

Hello, how are you? Fine thank you ... and you?

What a waste of time and breath. Save your breath, my mother used to say whenever she heard words being wasted. I think mom believed that in life you have a limited supply of words, and you shouldn't waste any of them on useless talk.

Useless talk is what this is all about. Many phone call conversations begin with the calling party saying, "Hello... how are you?"

The called party invariably and automatically responds with, "Fine thank you, and how are you?"

Now the caller is faced with the obligation to respond. He started this nonsense. Now he has been handed an affirmative obligation to respond.

I no longer do this, but when I did, it was at this point of the conversation that I would think to myself, "Why did I start this stupid dialog?"

First of all, the calling party really doesn't care how you are. Not only doesn't he care, but if you actually tell him how you are, before he realizes that he started this nonsense, he will be wondering why is this guy telling me about his prostate.

Now the other guy responds telling you about his colonoscopy.

If we assume each call of this kind wastes 20 seconds and there are 10 million of these calls a day in the

USA that's 200 million seconds, indeed a significant drain on the GDP.

Give me a break.

I'm saving mentioning the time wasted talking about the weather for another day. Maybe Tuesday, unless it rains, then Wednesday.

OK people; please stop wasting your breath with this nonsense. Consider the possibility mom was right. You only get so much breath and so many words to speak in life.

We've all experienced the final scene in a movie, or heard and read of instances in history and life and literature where someone is reaching for a last breath, grasping and gasping to get out some message about a secret formula, or confession, or words of love, or finding God, but fails to do so because he ran out of breath.

That's probably what mom was trying to tell us.

So this is why texting caught on so fast.

Save your breath. Smart lady my mom.

Snowflakes

There are no two identical snowflakes. Everybody learned that fact at age 4. I will refrain from mentioning how many snowflakes there are now, or have been everywhere it snows, from the beginning of time. Suffice to say, quite a few. So who's to say there are no two alike?

This is one of those subjects I don't have a lot to say about, but what I do have to say about it is pretty, pretty smart. I want the whole world to know, right here, right now; there are many identical snowflakes. Likely as many identical as not identical.

There I said it! You, dear reader, are among the first to know and you heard it here today from me.

The Italian Kitchen

A story about what I love about being Italian. A lot of it begins and ends with food and what goes on in Italian kitchens. This is a about an Italian man in an Italian kitchen.

It's important to note here that, back in the day, everything done in Italian kitchens was done by women. Actually I think it was a law in Connecticut. Until recently.

Anyway when women left the kitchen workforce and joined the real workforce, men moved in. At first reluctantly, knowing it is hard work. (That's why they let the ladies do it all those years).

But men in the kitchen caught on when men discovered all the cool kitchen tools available to use, making the job much easier. Men love tools and working with tools. As men started playing around inside, with kitchen tools, they discovered it was just as much fun as playing around with tools outside, or in the garage. Also your hands didn't get as dirty and in the wintertime it is warmer in the kitchen.

Another thing men discovered when preparing evening meals is that certain procedures can be employed to make the job easier and fun. My standard procedure involves using a basic tool found in every kitchen. The cork screw. Plan ahead so that the wine you open is either white or red depending which color you will use in preparing the meal.

Even if it's only a drop, every recipe can stand some wine, so it's good to have the open bottle right there on the counter as you work. My rule of thumb is to consume 42% of the opened wine while preparing the meal and the remaining 58% while enjoying the meal. Easy rule to remember.

After tasting the wine make sure the dishwasher is empty. I like loading the dishwasher as I go along so that by the time I sit down to eat most of the clean-up is out of the way and underway.

Working in the kitchen I prefer to have all the tools I will need and be using as well as all the food I'll be working with lined up out on the counter.

There are several must have kitchen tools for the Italian kitchen to be complete. First and foremost is the garlic press. It has only one purpose; it presses cloves of garlic into tiny moist morsels. After the cork screw this is the most important tool in an Italian kitchen. Need I say more? A variety of sharp kitchen knives for slicing and dicing, of course are a must. Spatulas, I love spatulas, all shapes and sizes, very handy kitchen tools. A tool you don't hear much about is the mezzaluna, that's Italian for a half moon shaped knife with two handles used to dice and mince. If you don't have one, get one. Having a mezzaluna is an Italian signal that you know what's cooking in the kitchen.

If you know what I mean.

A wooden spoon with a long handle is a favorite tool always nearby. I like wooden spoons, all kinds and shapes. I like the way wooden spoons feel in my hand and I like the way wooden spoons smell in the course of cooking, especially when stirring garlicy things. Garlicy smelling wooden spoons are a beautiful thing.

When it comes to down-right basic fundamental Italian kitchen ingredients, there are two. Garlic and olive oil.

I love to work with garlic, its taste, its smell, raw or cooked, and I love the feel of garlic in my hands as I peel and cut it into thin slices. When I'm preparing garlic, I sit at the counter taking the bulb apart, then separating each clove, then rolling it under the palm of my hand to loosen the skin to expose that little gem of goodness, periodically bringing my fingers up to my nostrils, to enjoy its fragrance. Like I said, I like, no make that love, everything about garlic. It's also good for you, health wise.

After garlic the next most important item in the Italian kitchen is olive oil. Here's something that may surprise you. Did you ever wonder how they get the olive pits out of the olives they squeeze to make olive oil? Well they don't. Olives are picked, washed and squeezed with the pits still inside the olive. As the olives, including pits are crushed, the first drippings dripping from the olive squeezing crushing machine is the extra virgin, followed by the next squeezed drippings, that's the regular virgin, and then comes the regular every day olive oil. Until I find out how crushed olive pits affect the taste I'm recommending extra virgin or virgin.

When I'm working in the kitchen I find it helpful to wear a cook's bib apron. I'm comfortable and confident if I look the part, like a chef. Especially if someone shows up to share the meal or just say hello.

All my recipes are in my head. I never really measure anything. I just do it as I go along. Like riding a bicycle, you don't actually think about it you just do it. That's me cooking, never quite the same, but always just a little bit different and a little bit better. I just get a feeling in my gut, when I'm adding garlic or wine or spices and parmesan, when enough is enough. It just occurred to me that there could be some connection between the gut feelings I get when I'm cooking and my gut where what I'm cooking is going to wind up. It's like magic.

If you know what I mean.

Don't Answer

An exercise for your brain.

I have a question. Who is the smartest person you know? Why?

I have no interest, *what so ever*, in the who of your answer. I'm suggesting you do this exercise in your head. I also recommend you not tell anyone your answers. Likely a bunch of people you know, are qualified to be considered. And included in that bunch, is at least one or two who are sure you would pick him or her as the one, if they knew what was going on it your head.

Who's the nicest person you know? Why? Same rules as above.

Here's a fun one, who's the wisest person you know?

While we are at it, who is the worst?

You must choose among people you know, really know. No historical, celebrity or criminal characters and the like. If you happen to be the smartest, or the wisest, or the nicest, go right ahead and pick yourself. Just don't tell anybody. Except maybe your mother.

I'm more interested in the whys. Is it possible for the same person to be the smartest and nicest? Also the smartest and the worst? But what about the nicest and the worst; is that possible?

OK, here's where I'm going with this; let's say you did the suggested exercise and listed the smartest, nicest, worst, any other adjective you can come up with. Is there anyone you could or would share that list with?

Who and why? If you share this list with anyone, then I suggest you are the dumbest.

The exercise is to think of each of these separate thoughts immediately and simultaneously as you read them and then immediately stop and forget about it. Now your brain is exercising and you are telling it to stop and forget it, but you can't, and that's more exercise.

There is an element of this kind of brain exercise in many of my stories.

Stories for exercising the brain.

Brain Clearing

Is it possible for a brain to explode?   In case you hear about my passing, check to see if the cause was brain explosion. My brain is chock-full of stories and things I want to write about.   They are rattling around in my noggin and I need to get them out and on paper. It's like a pin ball game going on in my head, I am about to tilt.

The problem is I don't have enough material on any one of these subjects to write a whole story, but I need to clear space in my brain. In my opinion what appears to be a sign of Alzheimer, is in fact nothing more than brain clutter. Years of accumulation, just like your attic, cellar, drawers and closets. Let the clearing begin, I need the space.

The subject I have the least amount of material to work with is about the pool water at my Florida condo.   One of the rules posted on a sign in the pool area states: "Drinking the pool water is not allowed." These words speak for themselves. Drinking the pool water is just plain not allowed.

Here's another thing I'd like to bounce off your brain while I'm cleaning out mine. When I arrive at my destination, and a song I like is playing on the car radio, I don't exit the car until the song ends. I need to know if anyone else does this.   Call or write.

In the category of weird things I've experienced, here's my Mystic Pizza story. It's got nothing to do with the movie of the same name. The event occurred 35 years ago while I was eating pizza in Mystic. Not at Mystic Pizza, but at a pizza place also in Mystic. In the course of eating pizza, I felt something foreign in my mouth. It felt like what you would feel if you cracked and broke off a piece of tooth.

Upon examination it looked like part of a tooth. With my tongue I felt around but could not find any indication that any of my teeth had fractured.

My dentist did a complete examination and confirmed the piece of tooth was not from any of my teeth. However he confirmed that what I found in my mouth was part of a human tooth. (That's it, nothing more to that story.)

Moving right along...clearing and cleaning.

It occurred to me that a couple of words, used in reference to women, have fallen out of favor. Broads and dames.

Nobody refers to women as broads and dames anymore. I don't recall ever hearing those words used in a derogatory manner. I thought it was kind of like a compliment. I remember the song from the Broadway Hit, South Pacific, "There Is Nothing Like a

Dame." Very complimentary to dames, if you ask me. Somehow broads and dames took offence at being called broads and dames.

A number of years ago, people reading the New York Times found that a lot of the paper's ink rubbed off on fingers and hands. For a time light weight gloves became available and were worn by readers. Then the print was improved and the inky hands problem was solved.

It occurred to me that if back then *the ink* could soil your skin, it is possible that there could be something in *the new and improved ink* that gets into New York Times reader's hands, winding up in the brain. Just saying.

I appreciate your help cleaning and clearing my brain. If you weren't reading this stuff, I wouldn't be writing, and if I wasn't writing my brain would explode. Thank you, keep reading.

Bend Over

There are direct and indirect reasons why old men choose to live in Florida during the winter months.

The most obvious direct reason is an abundance of healthy, warm, sunny days.

Indirectly, the warm climate makes it unnecessary to wear socks. Old men hate to wear socks, with good reason. They are hard to put on. Old men have a hard time bending over.

If you know what I mean.

Acts Of God

Everybody knows that property damage caused by Acts of God is not covered by insurance. Well everybody is wrong.

Hurricanes and lightning strikes are Acts of God. Hurricanes are windstorms. All basic property damage insurance policies cover windstorm and lightning damage.

I think I know how lack of insurance coverage for Acts of God got misunderstood.

Thousands of years ago whenever God showed up in person, he often caused lots of damage. Big stuff, fire and brimstone, Sodom and Gomorra, and don't forget Noah and the flood, just to mention a few of the major catastrophes that got media attention.

Even when he stopped showing up in person, his wrecking ball was bouncing around the world doing property damage. For sure, no insurance company would sell a policy to anyone with the power to cause catastrophic damage. You could only imagine how many claims there would be if God had liability insurance. Everybody and their brother would be suing God, not only for things he did, but for things he didn't do, like stop a storm or a war. Heaven on earth for plaintiff lawyers.

People who were damaged by God's recklessness knew better than to try to make a claim. Say you got a lawyer to go after flood damage to your house caused by heavy rain. God didn't need to send you a denial letter. He could just hit your house with a bolt of lightning. POW! House gone, house flood damage gone, end of story.

A market for protection from God developed. Someone figured out they could sell protection to cover the property damage He did every day. Property Insurance Coverage was invented. Thank God!

Even God liked the idea. He felt bad about some of his wraths, especially when they resulted in collateral damage. Little known fact: God loves insurance companies and helps them out whenever He can. Just think about the role He plays in the life insurance business.

Here's a thought, imagine if God owned a life insurance company. Buying life insurance from *God Life* would be a very smart move. It would be in God's best interest to see to it that you enjoyed a long prosperous life. The longer you live and prosper, the longer you will be paying annual premiums. In effect a Life Policy, from The God Life Insurance Company, would include, for no additional premium, the added benefit, actuarially speaking, of a long life existence.

If you know what I mean

Back to property damage: bottom line, you can buy coverage from an insurance company for protection from some kinds of property damage caused by Acts of God, like windstorms and lightning strikes.

However you cannot bring suit and collect directly from God. Acts of God are not covered *by God*. He is not insured. God is what lawyers refer to as judgement proof.

Amen.

The 3 Rs

In my lifetime I've crossed paths with 3 men who did something in their lifetime that definitely put them into the category of individuals I will not forget: Rodger, Ray D, and Red Ryder.

They couldn't be more different from each other. Actually one was a boy and two were men. Roger was a boy who at one time babysat my kids.

I never knew Ray D's last name; I just knew him as Ray D. He was the cook at a club where I hung out.

I'm not sure of the third guy's real name. He was a concert promoter. He had red hair. He promoted himself as Red Ryder. Red probably wasn't his real name. I doubt any mother would actually name her son Red just because his hair was red. You never know about things like that.

When my kids were young, we belonged to a pool and tennis club. Roger was, at the time, a teenager. There was nothing unusual about Roger. He was a friendly chubby kid. He was always around the pool hanging out with the kids. On several occasions, we hired Roger to babysit our kids.

Roger's father, Tom, was a nice friendly guy. I do remember that Roger and his dad didn't get along too well. Roger's old man was old fashioned, old school. Roger not so much.

I got to know Ray D pretty well because he was a cook at my favorite rock and roll club. I was into rock and roll. One thing about Ray D, he could whip up a mean Philly Cheese Steak Sandwich. Just the way I like it. Well done, not greasy. Raw onion, not cooked onion. You know most Philly Cheese Steak sandwiches come with cooked onions. But I like the onions raw. Just the way I am about onions.

One time, when I knew Ray D, it was my birthday. I decided to rent a stretch limo to pick up Linda, me and other couples I had invited to party with us. We were heading out to the club to start the celebration. Actually the celebration started as soon as we entered the limo in my driveway.

If you know what I mean.

Anyway on our way to the club, we pass a hitchhiker on the road. I realize the hitchhiker is Ray D. I tell the limo driver to pull over. We pick up Ray D. The driver said that was the first time he had ever picked up a hitchhiker while driving a limo. No doubt Ray D was surprised when the limo pulled over to pick him up. I did a lot of hitchhiking when I was a kid, about 10,000 miles worth. Never once was I picked up by a limo.

The limo was already pretty crowded. Ray D winds up sitting in the spot Linda was sitting in; Linda winds up sitting on Ray D's lap.

Linda knew Ray D, but she didn't know him as well as I did. Mostly she was home with the kids when I was hanging out at the club. She knew him enough to know she didn't like him too much. She wasn't happy about picking him up in the limo, especially the part about sitting on his lap.

I met Red Ryder because, as an aficionado of rock and roll, I wanted to get into the business of promoting rock concerts. I stumbled on to some info about an outdoor concert being planned for a nearby town. I made contact with Red Ryder. I attended meetings and invested a few bucks. Wow! I'm a concert promotor.

Not so fast. I wind up in charge of parking. I'm the parking attendant at the concert. Not exactly what I had in mind. I say goodbye to Red and retire from the concert promotion business. In case you're wondering, I did not meet any groupies.

By now you figured out that what Roger, Ray and Red have in common is that their first initial is R.

True, but unfortunately there's more to the story.

Roger got into an argument with his father, Tom, nice guy. Roger killed Tom with a baseball bat. As far as I know, Roger never played Little League or any baseball. But he had a bat. I don't know if he had a glove.

Ray D raped and murdered a nurse. Actually first he was accused of raping a nurse. He was tried and acquitted. Later he killed a different nurse. He cut her up in a bathtub. It was a long time ago. I'm pretty sure it was a different nurse, because you would not expect the nurse he raped to be back

hanging around with Ray D. But you never know.
Safe to say, Ray D had a fondness for nurses.

Many years after I retired from the concert business,
I read a story in the newspaper about Red Ryder.
Red was in the back seat of a taxi when he got into an
argument with the driver. From the back seat, Red
shot the cab driver 3 times in the back. Red claimed
he shot the cab driver in self-defense!

Eating Grandma

Being retired, I spend a lot of time sitting by the pool in the Florida sunshine. There are things I have been pondering for years. Sometimes, all of a sudden, into my head pop answers to a couple of my oldest ponderings.

Like, for example, about UFOs. Since I was a kid, I thought a lot about UFOs and visitors from outer space. I mean there are so many billions of galaxies, there must be some *thing* sufficiently advanced to schedule a check in with Earth. I could never figure out why nobody ever succeeded in getting a good picture of a UFO or their crew once they landed. Actually what I concluded was that UFO activity was mostly in remote areas, and there just didn't happen to be anyone around with a camera. Kind of like a coincidence.

Another idea I had was that ETs just aren't attractive enough to want any photos taken. In every drawing or picture of ETs I've seen, they are pretty ugly. Although you would think they would like to show off close-ups of their space ships; at least the outside. I could understand them not wanting you to get inside the ship. It probably smells bad anyway, from such a long trip.

While sitting by the pool, I figured it out.

It just popped into my head. I wasn't even thinking about anything in particular when it occurred to me that there are about two billion cell phones in the world capable of taking pictures; still no good UFO/ET pictures.

Not only are there no good UFO/ET pictures, but the numbers of the not so good UFO/ET pictures, that used to become available, from time to time, are also way down.

My pondering this question is finished.

I have concluded that there are no UFO visitors.

Unless they are invisible then that's another story.

Another thing I've been wondering and pondering about is the organization known as PETA - People for The Ethical Treatment of Animals. I think I figured out what's cooking with them. They are very passionate about their cause. I never heard anybody explain the real reason they feel the way they do. This is what I have concluded: It is very possible most PETA people believe in Reincarnation. They figure their coming back in a next life as some animal or a dog or cat. This could account for the devotion pet owners have for their pets, very understandable.

What I'm talking about here is that the more serious believers on this subject are thinking there's a chance some of us could come back as pigs or steers; bacon or steak. I might also mention chickens and fish, because I know someone who won't eat anything that has a face. I bet you never heard that one. Well I did, and I offer it here to share that morsel of info with you. You are welcome.

So a PETA member in good standing is concerned, as well they should be, that some family members who have already bought the farm, so to speak, have made it back to the farm.

If you know what I mean.

That pork roast or porterhouse could be your Grandmother.

Nobody I know wants to eat their Grandmother.

Then I started to wonder why was it that the answers to these two ponderings popped into my head at the same time on the same day while sitting by the pool. After taking several readings, my wondering about ponderings revealed to me how, my fairly sound brain works. Here's the connection with UFO's and eating Grandma.

About 65 years ago, when I was 13, I see on TV an episode of "Twilight Zone". A space ship comes to Earth with very friendly visitors. They offer to us Earthlings a copy of their Good Book. Someone at Yale, or maybe it was Harvard, gets the job of trying to decode and translate what the visitors Good Book says.

Meanwhile, the very friendly visitors have convinced some of our people to go back with them to their deliciously described planet. As the last of a bunch of our people who opted to go, are boarding the space ship, and as the ramp door is closing, the guy who was working on the translation, is running across the field, waving a copy of their Good Book in his hand

and shouting, "IT'S A COOK BOOK" "IT'S A COOK BOOK"

So now we know how my brain works, and I willingly share it with you.

You are welcome!

Experience

This is an old story: Stop me if you've heard it.

A building owner is having trouble with a finicky boiler that is used to heat his building. Attempts by plumbers, electricians and heating specialists, fail to isolate the problem and repair the boiler.

Then one day he hires a Boiler Man, who he has heard is the Best Boiler Repairman in the business.

The Boiler Man shows up at the building and proceeds to inspect the boiler. After about 5 minutes looking at and listening to the boiler, he reaches into his pocket and takes out a little monkey wrench. He goes around to the side and taps the boiler 3 times.

He tells the owner the boiler is fixed and he leaves. Sure enough the boiler is running like new. No more finicky problems.

A month later the building owner gets the bill. It's $900. He calls the Boiler Man to protest the amount. "How can you charge me $900? You were here 5 minutes with a little wrench and all you did was tap the boiler 3 times." How do you justify $900?

The Boiler Man's response, "I knew where to tap."

Elaine's Knuckles

In 1946 my third grade teacher was Miss Driscoll, I was 8.

Elaine, a classmate, is seated next to me in the classroom.

I can tell this story now because it happened 70 years ago, and the Statute of Limitations has run on the *criminal acts* I am about to reveal.

I should also mention that Elaine and me, (I know I, but I like me), were not what you would call the best of friends. She lived on the first floor of the 3 family house right next door to the house I lived in. Another classmate, Peggy, lived on the third floor. Peggy and me, we were very friendly, even at 8, Elaine and Peggy, not so much.

If you know what I mean.

Are you getting the picture here? Actually Peggy has nothing to do with this story and I'm sorry I mentioned her.

Now back in the classroom, Miss Driscoll and Elaine have issues. Elaine's not doing her work. Whatever the work kids in the third grade are supposed to do, Elaine wasn't doing. Because I sit next to her in class, Miss Driscoll deputizes and directs me, to keep an eye on her and keep her working.

One evening my Mom gets a call from Elaine's mom, reporting that I am whacking her daughter on her knuckles with a 12 inch wooden ruler.

I don't think Elaine told her mother it was a 12 inch ruler. She probably never noticed that the ruler in question was 12 inches. Although she probably did know it was a wooden ruler. Eight year old girls in 1946 might not know 12 inches from 15 inches, but they would know wood when they see it.

When my mom confronts me with the story I confirm and confess that I have been deputized by Miss Driscoll to reach over and whack Elaine on her knuckles with the wooden ruler whenever I notice she is not "doing her work." I can't remember what the *work* that she was supposed to be doing was, but accurate to say that whenever I noticed that she wasn't doing it, I whacked her on the knuckles.

For the record: I was authorized by Miss Driscoll to whack her on the knuckles. Miss Driscoll supplied the 12 inch wooden ruler. I was only doing what I was told to do, your Honor.

I don't recall the details. Somehow it all got worked out. Miss Driscoll confirmed my story and continued to teach third grade for decades. Nobody got arrested. I don't recall any other contact with Elaine. I do recall further contact with Peggy, but that's another story.

If you know what I mean.

Telephone Brave

Do you ever get the feeling on phone calls, that the person talking with you is sounding just a little strange? Nothing you can put your finger on, but you notice wordiness or sentence structure just a bit differently than you experience normally with this caller. Sometimes it's in the pitch or the volume or the articulation.

What I'm suggesting here is the possibility that someone, at the *speaker's* location, is listening in on that conversation. The speaker knows his words are being overheard, his remarks are being tailored to accommodate *that listener*.

I'm not implying that there is necessarily anything surreptitious going on in this particular call. I do this all the time. My reason is that the person hearing the call, on my end, may have questions about the conversation they are overhearing. I try to tailor my words to minimize the fallout from the call. I hope to avoid having to repeat the entire conversation I just completed. That is accomplished, if most of the part of the conversation not heard by the overhearing party, can be gleaned from the part they did hear.

If you know what I mean.

Now there is another kind of telephone call where the words coming through to your end are abrupt, professional in tone, and sometimes even hostel. Much different than when you met and spoke about the very same subject in person. You may wonder, what changed since we last spoke?

Some callers will say things to you in a phone call, that they would not say to your face. These are the callers I refer to as being *telephone brave*. Often this call is being made on a business matter, to deny a request, deliver bad news, or ask for the past due payment.

Often calls of this kind are being overheard and directed by the caller's boss. Don't forget, all calls are recorded, *for training purposes*.

If you know what I mean.

Up There

I have no proof that God or Heaven exist. However, just in case they do exist, I feel obliged to share some thoughts I have about what may be going on up there.

My intention is to get you thinking about some of the things you may need to deal with if you do manage to show up, up there.

Location, location, location, Heaven is a nice place. Blue sky, sunshine gentle breeze, 80 degrees, low humidity, white sandy beaches, beautiful flowers, grass and music. Kinda like Florida in the winter months.

Heaven is a very busy place. Even in today's crazy world, many millions of souls a day check in, up there. Back in the day, before ethics and morality expired, it was even busier. But I digress.

Whatever the number is, it's big. The billions of souls are scattered far and wide. I check in at the Gate Office, punch in my SS number and get connected into the cloud.

It occurs to me that the first thing I would want to find out if I got up there is, who do I know who got up there before me? We are all pretty sure mom made the cut, and probably dad too. The software program is so cool; in a short time you know who's there and who's not there, but not why they're not there.

If you know what I mean.

The purpose of this epistle is to get you thinking, who would you want to see first and why? If each visit was allotted just a few minutes, you may want to clean up the messy ones first. You know the ones where you get balled out for the mistakes you made on the way getting up there.

On the other hand, if there are no time limits, you may want to talk to the ones you missed the most in life. After mom and dad, I'd next want to speak to the ones I thought could give me the most detail on what's going on up there. How to work the system, if there is a system.

Next on my list are questions about diet and exercise. What possible reason could there be to diet and exercise?

If you know what I mean.

The food thing is big with me. I like to eat, I know what I like. Is there pizza? Do they offer Italian? Is it cafeteria style or buffet? What about the kitchen hours. I like to eat late. Can I see a menu?

I'm also concerned about the music. I can put up with a little church music, very little. Absolutely no Rap!

Who do you call with complaints about Heaven? Imagine if after working your whole life to get up there, when you got up there, you didn't like the music or the food?

That would be Hell.

Am I the only one who thinks about these things sitting in the sun by the pool enjoying the breeze, the flowers and especially the grass.

If you know what I mean.

Write Away

If you can find a handful of people who like what you write, you are a writer.

Go ahead, write away to your heart's content.

Wait! Stop! Hold the presses!

I just changed my mind about that opening sentence. See what a wonderful thing being a writer is; you can just change your mind, start again, no complaints, no one, except you, saw it. Zap; it's gone, start over. I am sharing this writing secret with you, dear reader friend. (I know, in your mind, you are thanking me.) You're welcome.

What I now want to open with is this: If you can find a handful of readers who like *the way* you write, then you are a writer.

So it's not about *the what*, it's about *the way*. The way is not just about how you put words together side-by-side to make a sentence; it's also about how you plant within those side-by-side words something else.

That something else, if you catch it right, will cause the readers brain to engage. Once engaged, the brain begins to question and deduce. The question is, where is the writer going with this? About the same time that question pops into the reader's mind, the mind, to some extent on its own, goes into deduction mode searching for a reasoned conclusion. The reader and his mind are hooked into the developing story.

Starting with the title, and every word thereafter, strive to create chaos in the reader's mind. The title itself should spark attention, the kind of attention that will cause the reader, from the first word he reads, to start searching for what the title has to do with the story.

As you continue writing, start planting, at first little twists and turns and facts that may or may not have anything to do with where you are going. Remember, you as a literary licensed writer, can insert any crazy thing that comes into your head. If you come to a fork in the road take it. Use that fork to hint at where you are planning to go. Then if the spirit moves you, forget where you hinted you were going and go someplace else. After wandering around for a few paragraphs, scrambling the readers brain, get back to the title story.

The readers scrambled brain cells are exhausted, they have no idea where this craziness is going. (Message from brain cells to writer...lead on.)

My original interest in writing was solely to tell my stories to my kids and grandkids. It never occurred to me that anyone else would be interested in anything I had to say about anything. And my kids probably wouldn't be interested until I'm dead. No man is a prophet in his own land and time.

If you know what I mean.

Reliving the stories of my experiences, in my head, felt very exciting; when it came to writing them down chronologically, I just couldn't do it. Exciting in my head but boring to write. I saw this movie; I know how each story ends.

So I sign up for a writing class. The assignment for each class is to write two pages about anything. My mind was free to fly and write away; the take-off was exciting from the start. Any crazy nonsense ideas bouncing around in my brain began to leak out through my fingers onto the page. No limits. I found I was free to tell my mostly true stories in a fun literary license crazy flowing way.

The leaks became a flood, the crazier the better. I found I could write the way I talk, which is the way I think or maybe it is the other way around.

Surprise, surprise, now I was having fun, actual fun, writing. Who knew this would be possible. Ideas of unusual fun ways to say and write stuff coming to me, pouring out faster than I can type.

Initially a handful of mentally stable adults, mostly classmates in Florida, liked my stuff. When I got back to Connecticut, another handful of readers said nice things and asked to see more. I am on a roll planning to deliver, marrying my writing style to unusual subjects.

I found my biggest concern was could I find a way to write what I was thinking, in my head, so that the reader would enjoy reading as much as I enjoyed writing. The fun part for me is writing the way I am thinking which may not be the way the reader's mind is thinking.

Quirky thinking is my way of thinking; it's like the Escher optical illusion staircase going up, going down; can the reader follow along without getting annoyed?

So there you have it. I really don't care if you like what I write about. What I do care about is if the way I write is as much fun for you reading it, as it is for me writing it; so much so that even if you have no interest in my subject, are bored by it or even hate it, you, dear reader, continue on because having enjoyed reading some of my other stuff, you are curious, more than curious, anxiously awaiting, anticipating, trying to guess what nonsense is this nut case planning to write/say/do next. Where is this story going, and when he does make a point will I understand and appreciate the quirky craziness of not what he said, but how he said it.

OK that's it, enough said by me on this subject. And since I fancy myself a writer in accordance with the definition herein described, remember that I can change my mind and change everything I said. You can take this story with a Grain of Salt, whatever that means.

Speaking of salt, I'd like to mention, if salt was a color, any color, say red, when you used the salt shaker you would know how much salt you shook out. Like pepper is black and you can see how much you shook out. With white salt you never know. Different shakers have different size holes; it's easy to get it wrong. But if salt was red, you would know right off the bat. I know some readers won't understand what right off the bat means, so to simplify and tie this whole story together from beginning to end, I will, in my capacity as a writer, rewrite and change that final line

From: With red salt you would know right off the bat

To: With red salt you would know Write Away.

If you know what I mean.

About the author

John Apicella is a Licensed Public Insurance Adjuster, retired from the firm he founded in 1976. That firm, Apicella Adjusters, Inc., based in Connecticut, is family owned and operated. John and his wife Linda are Florida residents. They have three grown children and two grandchildren.

Email: John@IfyouknowwhatImean.net

50476770R00067

Made in the USA
Columbia, SC
11 February 2019